Planet Earth

Rainforests

Steve Parker

QED Publishing

QED

Copyright © QED Publishing 2008

First published in the UK in 2008 by
QED Publishing
A Quarto Group company
226 City Road
London EC1V 2TT

www.qed-publishing.co.uk

A catalogue record for this book is available from
the British Library.

Printed and bound in China

ISBN 978 1 84835 059 5

Author Steve Parker
Design and Editorial East River Partnership

Publisher Steve Evans
Creative Director Zeta Davies

Words in **bold** are
explained in the glossary
on page 30.

Contents

Rain and forest

Rainforests are well named. They have lots of tall trees, close together, and it rains and rains and rains!

Warm and wet

Rainforests are wet nearly all year round. Although there may be a short dry season lasting a few weeks, it rains almost every day, week after week. **Tropical** rainforests are not only wet, they are also very warm. The temperature is at least 20ºC on most days, and sometimes higher than 30ºC.

Rainforest trees grow close together, forming a thick, green covering.

The rare Asiatic lion now lives only in India's Gir rainforest.

Wow!

Although rainforests cover only one-sixteenth of the Earth's land area, they are home to more than half of all animals, plants and other living things.

Mangrove trees grow along some tropical coasts.

Plants and animals

Living things grow fast in a tropical rainforest's damp, steamy warmth. There are lots of amazing plants, from tiny flowers to enormous trees. Animals of every kind also live here, including worms and bugs, colourful frogs, screeching birds, huge elephants, leaping monkeys and shy gorillas.

It's so... wet!

Some rainforests get more than five times the rain in New York City, eight times more rain than London and fifteen times more than Los Angeles.

Rainforest people get food from plants in the forest.

5

Types of rainforests

Rainforests grow mainly around the middle of the world, on either side of the equator. This area is called the tropics, where it is warm all year.

NORTH AMERICA

Central America

Amazon

SOUTH AMERICA

Water vapour

As winds blow over oceans, they take up water. Winds do not carry water as a liquid, but as **vapour** that floats in the air and cannot be seen. The vapour makes the winds feel damp. When these winds blow over land, the water vapour changes into drops of water. These clump together to form clouds and fall as rain. Rainforest grow where there is most rain.

Wow!

Each year, it rains on about 120 days in New York City, 180 days in London and more than 300 days in some rainforests.

It's so... cool!

The average temperature in rainforests in the south of New Zealand's South Island is just 9°C. Some tropical rainforests are three times hotter than this.

Clouds blowing in from the sea keep rainforests wet and steamy.

■ Temperate rainforests

■ Tropical rainforests

South-east Asia

Japan

The biggest rainforest areas are in South America, Africa and South-east Asia.

Philippines

Sumatra

Borneo

EQUATOR

Java

New Guinea

CA

Madagascar

Australia

New Zealand

Warm and cool

Tropical rainforests near the **equator** are warm all year, and have the most plants and animals. There are **temperate** rainforests in cooler places, such as along the western coast of North America and on the island of Tasmania.

7

Layers of the rainforest

From the ground to the treetops, a rainforest has different layers where all sorts of animals and plants live.

Dim and quiet

If you walk though a rainforest, you notice that the forest floor is a dim and quiet place. Few flowers grow, and most animals that live here hide away. Not far above are the tops of tall bushes, shrubs and young trees. This is the understorey layer.

It's so... scary!

The world's biggest spider lives on the rainforest floor in South America. The goliath tarantula is too big to sit on a dinner plate!

Wow!

In the emergent layer, the tallest trees tower high above the canopy layer, at more than 60 metres in height.

The strangler fig is a killer! It grows up a tree trunk, forms a tube around it and slowly kills the tree.

Busy and noisy

The **canopy layer** of a rainforest is a tangle of branches, twigs, leaves, flowers and fruits. It is a busy and noisy place, as most rainforest animals live here. Further up, there are taller trees. These form the **emergent layer**, where monkeys and eagles look across the rainforest.

Rainforest are split into four different layers.

Emergent layer

Canopy layer

Understorey layer

Forest floor

Rainforest animals

Rainforests are full of creatures, many of which hide away and are difficult to find.

Slimy trails

Rainforests are home to many types of animal. Most common are small insects, such as flies, ants and termites. Brightly coloured butterflies fly between flowers, and snails and slugs leave slimy trails.

Swinging monkeys

The agile spider monkey, which lives in South American rainforests, swings from tree to tree using its hands, feet and tail to grab and hold branches. Below, fish and turtles swim in pools and swamps.

Spider monkeys feast on fruits and flowers.

Wow!

The biggest tree-dwelling animal is the orang-utan of South-east Asia. A fully grown male can weigh 80 kilograms – as much as a person.

It's so huge!

The world's biggest snakes live in rainforests. In Africa and Asia, enormous pythons swallow **prey** that is sometimes the size of a pig!

The jaguar's spotted coat helps it to hide in the shadows of the forest.

Screeching toucans

Rainforests are also home to cats of all sizes. The marbled cat of Asia looks like a tiny leopard, while the jaguar of South America is almost as big as a lion. In the trees, parrots, macaws and toucans screech and flap between the branches.

Toucans crack nuts with their huge bill.

Male crickets chirp to attract females.

Sounds of the rainforest

The rainforest can be one of the noisiest places in the natural world, especially at dawn and dusk.

Howler monkeys roar to protect their territory.

Day and night

Sometimes the rainforest is quiet. In the middle of the day, and for most of the night, many animals rest. At dawn and dusk, it is very different. Gibbons whoop, monkeys holler, birds chirrup, frogs croak, crickets and cicadas chirp and flies and bees buzz.

Hyacinth macaws squawk
warnings to other
members of their flock.

The loudest animal
for its size is the cicada.
If this insect was as big
as a person, its chirps
could be heard
20 kilometres away!

Wow!

Attracting partners

Many of the larger creatures make sounds to defend their territory. This is the area of forest where they live and feed. Their calls warn others to stay away. Animals, such as frogs, crickets and birds, make special songs and sounds at breeding time to attract partners.

It's so... loud!

The world's loudest land animals are South American howler monkeys. Their whoops carry for 5 kilometres through the treetops.

Moving through the trees

Most rainforest animals live in the branches of the rainforest canopy. They have different ways of moving around the trees.

Twisting and turning

Flying is a great way to travel through, and over, the rainforest. Eagles soar above the canopy looking for prey, such as monkeys and sloths. Hawks twist and turn among the branches to grab smaller birds. At night, bats snap up insects and owls swoop down on mice and lizards.

Some flying lizards can glide up to 100 metres, using their tail to steer.

Fastest mover

One of the fastest rainforest movers is the gibbon. It swings from tree to tree using its long, powerful arms, hanging by its hook-like hands.

Gliding around

Some rainforest animals that seem to fly are really gliding through the air. Flying lizards, flying squirrels, flying frogs and flying snakes all use large flaps of parachute-like body skin to glide around.

Gibbons have curved hands and feet to grip branches.

It's so small!

The world's smallest mammal is the bumblebee bat of South-east Asia. With a body as small as a bumblebee, this tiny bat weighs less than a British 1p coin.

Wow!

The best glider is the flying lemur, or colugo, of South-east Asia. It is not a true flier, nor a lemur. But it can glide for more than 150 metres.

Deadly killers

Rainforest creatures are always on the lookout for danger. There could be a killer on the next branch!

Deadly poisons

Not all killers are big. Many rainforest spiders, centipedes and scorpions use poisonous bites or stings to kill their prey. Some tiny South American frogs have deadly poisons in their skin, and bright colours to warn other creatures not to eat them! Local people tip their blowdarts, arrows and spears with this poison.

The poison from one bite of a king cobra can kill an elephant.

Tiny poison arrow frogs are only as long as your thumb.

Wow!

The poison in the skin of one poison arrow frog is so powerful it could kill up to 20 people!

Large predators

Some of the world's most powerful **predators** live in rainforests. The largest big cat is the tiger, which stalks Asian rainforests for deer and wild pigs. In South America, the caiman lurks near swamps and snaps up turtles and fish. Growing up to 250 kilograms, the Amazon's green anaconda is the world's heaviest snake.

Tigers are the largest hunters in the rainforest.

Caimans catch fish, turtles and crabs.

It's so... poisonous!

The king cobra of Asia is the world's longest poisonous snake. It grows to be more than 5 metres long, and its favourite food is other snakes!

Rainforest trees

Some of the world's tallest, heaviest and fastest-growing trees are found in rainforests.

Life in a tree

Thousands of creatures depend on a rainforest tree. Caterpillars munch its leaves, hummingbirds sip nectar from its flowers, monkeys eat its fruits and birds nest in holes in its trunk. There are teak trees in Asia, mahogany trees in Africa and Central America and rosewood trees around the world. The kapok tree of Central and South America grows to be 70 metres tall. That is the same height as an 18-storey building.

Emerald tree boas wrap themselves around branches and wait for prey.

It's so... sticklike!

Giant stick insects found in South-east Asia are the world's longest insects. Some are 30 centimetres in length, and 55 centimetres with their legs stretched out.

Using camouflage

Some animals depend so much on trees, they look like them! Stick insects, or 'walking sticks', resemble twigs. Leaf insects and the tree boa snake are green, just like leaves. The colourful flower mantis is disguised as a flower. Looking like part of the surroundings to avoid being seen is called **camouflage**.

Insects slip into a pitcher plant and are digested.

Rosewood trees are under threat from loggers who cut them for their sweet-smelling wood.

Wow!

A few rainforest flowers grow high above the forest floor, sometimes 50 metres up in the forks of great trees.

Cooktown orchids grow in rainforests in north-eastern Australia.

The teeming canopy

In the rainforest canopy, twigs, stems, buds, blossom, fruits and seeds provide food for a huge variety of animals.

Bird life

Colourful small birds, such as sunbirds, honeyeaters and motmots, fly among branches in the rainforest. The great hornbill of South Asia has a wingspan of 1.6 metres and a huge **casque** on its head. The world's biggest eagles, the harpy eagle of Central and South America and the Philippine eagle, prey on monkeys, sloths, snakes and birds.

The great hornbill digs out insects from trees with its powerful beak.

Morpho butterflies find sunny clearings to warm themselves.

Pygmy marmosets live on the sap of rainforest trees.

Sloths sleep for 16 hours each day.

Hanging around

Some animals that live in the canopy never come down to the ground. These include monkeys, tree rats and lizards, such as iguanas and geckos. One of the slowest creatures in the canopy is the sloth. This leaf eater hangs from branches by its long curved claws, sometimes spending an entire week feeding on one tree.

It's so... little!

Marmosets are little South American rainforest monkeys. The smallest is the pygmy marmoset, with a head and body as small as a human fist.

The rafflesia plant has no leaves.

The forest floor

Some of the world's biggest and most exciting animals slip through the shadows of the rainforest floor.

Forest elephants live in small groups.

The forest okapi is a relative of the giraffe.

Moving silently

Elephants may seem easy to spot but, in West Africa, forest elephants move almost silently among the trees, hardly noticed in the gloom. Lowland gorillas, the world's biggest apes, also live here. These gentle creatures eat leaves and fruits. Tapirs are pig-like animals with a long, bendy nose. They live in South American and Asian rainforests.

The tapir's fleshy nose helps it to grab soft, tasty leaves.

WOW!

The capybara, a huge cousin of the guinea pig, lives in South American rainforests. Weighing more than 60 kilograms, it is the world's largest rodent.

Darkness below

The floor of the rainforest gets little light because of the thick canopy high above. Few small plants are able to survive on the ground. Only when a huge tree has fallen down will sunlight break through. Then the seeds of flowers, bushes and trees can grow.

It's so... smelly!

At one metre wide, the rafflesia of South-east Asia is the world's largest flower. It attracts flies to carry its **pollen** by smelling of rotting meat!

Mountain forests

Not all rainforests are found on flat lowlands. Some have developed on the sides of steep hills and mountains.

Furry gorillas

Tropical mountain rainforests grow high up. In these regions, it is not only very wet, but also cooler than in tropical lowlands. Here, animals have thick fur to keep warm. The furry mountain gorillas that live in Central Africa sleep in trees at night. Mother gorillas bend branches together to make a nest for themselves and their babies. Big male gorillas, which can weigh more than 200 kilograms, sleep in grassy nests on the ground.

A big male gorilla, or silverback, will protect his family group.

It's so... rare!

With just a few hundred left, the mountain gorilla is one of the world's rarest big animals.

Bamboo eater

The spectacled bear of South America lives in rainforests that are 2500 metres high in the Andes mountains. This bear eats almost any food, plant or animal. The giant panda from the cool, damp, cloudy hills of south-east China, however, prefers to eat just one kind of food. It rarely eats anything other than bamboo.

Spectacled bears can sniff out food hidden in the canopy.

Wow!

A fully grown giant panda is bigger than a person. A newborn giant panda, however, is tiny. It weighs about 100 grams, less than an apple.

Pandas have strong teeth to bite through bamboo.

Cool rainforests

Not all of the world's rainforests are warm and wet. Many are cool and wet and are home for an amazing range of plants and animals.

Tallest trees

Rainforests in cooler regions are known as temperate rainforests. Although cool, these forests teem with life. They have the world's tallest trees, such as redwoods in America and kauri pines in New Zealand. These trees are called **evergreens**. This means that they keep their leaves all year, and their seeds grow in **cones**.

Many cooler rainforests grow on hills and mountains.

Wow!

The kakapo is a large New Zealand parrot. It cannot fly, it feeds at night and there are fewer than 90 left alive. Scientists have given each one a name.

Birds and beavers

The floor of a temperate forest is wet and is covered with ferns, mosses and creepers. Strange animals live in these cool rainforests, including the flightless kiwi bird of New Zealand and the mountain beaver of North America.

It's so... tall!

Cool rainforests have some of the tallest trees in the world. North American redwoods, Tasmanian giant gum trees and New Zealand kahikateas, or white pines, reach more than 70 metres in height.

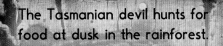
The Tasmanian devil hunts for food at dusk in the rainforest.

The blue duiker is 30 centimetres tall — the same as a small dog.

Powerful bite

The blue duiker is a small, shy antelope that lives in the cool forests of central and southern Africa. The stocky Tasmanian devil is an aggressive and noisy forest creature that has one of the most powerful bites of all mammals.

Disappearing rainforests

Orang-utans may be extinct in 30 years.

Rainforests are the richest places in the world for wildlife. But they are also places that are most at risk, and are disappearing fast.

Laws against illegal logging are often ignored.

Destroying trees

Rainforests face many dangers, especially in the tropics. Here, trees are cut down for their strong timber, which is known as hardwood. With no trees left, many forest animals then have no homes. With no tree roots, forest soil gets washed away by heavy rain and blocks nearby rivers.

Cleared for crops

Rainforests are being cleared by fire to grow farm crops, such as sugar cane and oil palm trees. Many areas are also being planted with grass to feed cows and other **livestock**. Some rainforest animals are in danger because they are hunted for their meat.

Once the forest has been cleared, the land is used to grow crops.

Saving rainforests

All kinds of rainforest animals are at great risk, from butterflies and beetles to tigers, gorillas and rhinos. We must work hard to save rainforests, with their wonderful plants and amazing creatures.

Wow!
An area of rainforest the size of a soccer pitch is cut down every second.

The Javan rhino is almost extinct in the wild.

Glossary

Camouflage Colours and patterns that blend with the surroundings, making a creature hard to see.

Canopy layer The main level of branches, leaves and flowers in a rainforest, high above the ground.

Casque A helmet-like head covering.

Cone Hard, woody parts made by trees, such as pines and firs, which contain seeds.

Dusk The time around sunset, between day and night.

Emergent layer The tallest trees in a forest, above the main canopy layer.

Equator An imaginary line around the middle of the world, midway between the North Pole and South Pole.

Evergreen Trees that have some leaves all through the year.

Livestock Animals kept by people, especially on farms, such as cows, sheep and pigs.

Pollen Tiny, dust-like grains that must get from the male parts of a flower to the female parts so that seeds can start to form.

Predator An animal that hunts others for food.

Prey An animal that is hunted for food.

Temperate Places where it is neither very hot nor very cold, usually with warm summers and cool winters.

Territory An area where an animal lives, feeds and raises young, which it defends against others of its kind.

Tropical Around the middle of the world, in the region called the tropics, where it is very warm all year.

Understorey layer Bushes, shrubs, young trees and other low-growing plants in a forest.

Vapour Visible form of moisture floating in the air. Fog and steam are vapours.

Index

AMY BLAKEMORE Photographs 1988–2008

Alison de Lima Greene
with Anne Wilkes Tucker,
Chrissie Iles, and
Marisa C. Sánchez

The Museum of Fine Arts, Houston
Distributed by Yale University Press, New Haven and London

This catalogue was published to coincide with the exhibition *Amy Blakemore: Photographs 1988–2008* at the Museum of Fine Arts, Houston, May 9–September 13, 2009.

Publications Director: Diane Lovejoy
Editorial Manager: Heather Brand
Designed by Emily Hoops Sanders
Reproduction photographer: Thomas R. DuBrock
Printed in the United States of America

Distributed by Yale University Press,
New Haven and London
www.yalebooks.com

Front cover illustration: Amy Blakemore, *Jill in Woods,* 2005, chromogenic photograph, 19 x 19 inches (48.3 x 48.3 cm)

Back cover illustration: Amy Blakemore, *Swing,* 1992, gelatin silver photograph, 15 x 15 inches (38.1 x 38.1 cm)

Library of Congress Cataloging-in-Publication Data

Blakemore, Amy, 1958–
    Amy Blakemore : photographs 1988–2008 / Alison de Lima Greene with Anne Wilkes Tucker, Chrissie Iles, and Marisa C. Sánchez.
        p. cm.
    Includes bibliographical references.
    Summary: "Presents a twenty-year survey of the black-and-white and color photographs of Amy Blakemore, taken with a Diana camera, accompanied by four essays and an interview with the artist"—Provided by publisher.
    ISBN 978-0-300-14699-8 (pbk. : alk. paper)
    1. Photography, Artistic. 2. Blakemore, Amy, 1958– I. Greene, Alison de Lima. II. Title. III. Title: Photographs 1988–2008.
    TR655.B55 2009
    770.92—dc22
                                            2008051615

This book is dedicated in memory of Robert T. and Mary Tippin Blakemore

—Amy Blakemore, 2009

SPONSORS

Amy Blakemore: Photographs 1988–2008
has been organized by the Museum of Fine
Arts, Houston.

Major sponsorship is provided by:

Mr. and Mrs. Michael C. Linn

**Generous funding is provided by
the Friends of Amy Blakemore:**

The Bequest of Edward B. Mayo
Leslie and Jack Blanton, Jr.
Leslie and Brad Bucher
Sara Paschall Dodd-Spickelmier
    and Keith Spickelmier
Dillon Kyle and Sam Lasseter
Carey C. Shuart
Mary and George Hawkins
Nancy Powell Moore
The Alice Kleberg Reynolds Foundation
Dr. and Mrs. Byron York
Phyllis and George Finley
Charlotte and Bill Ford
Allyson Hancock Kinzel and Jason B. Kinzel
Karen McClure and Jeff Post

Iman Saqr
Denby Auble and Kerry Inman
Cynthia Morgan Batmanis
Deborah Bay and Edgar Browning
Mary Kay and Bob Casey
Keith Forman and Mary Morton
Lynn Goode
Mr. and Mrs. Stephen J. Gross
Kathy Oliver
Christopher E. Vroom
Jill Whitten and Robert Proctor
Clinton T. Willour

Additional support is provided by:

Rebecca A. Bratton
David N. Britton
Shelley Calton
Susanne Devich and Lee Bergman
Anne Ribble
Edie Stavinoha
Betsy Haas
Mary Murrey and Michael Ittmann
Tom Oldham
Valerie Owhadi

CONTENTS

FOREWORD

In the autumn of 1982 the Museum of Fine Arts, Houston (MFAH), inaugurated the Core Program, inviting artists for one- and two-year residencies at the museum's Glassell School of Art. Conceived as a laboratory for research and experimentation by Allan Hacklin, then director of the school, and Rachel Hecker, assistant director, the Core Program established an open and critical environment that encouraged young artists to break new ground and refine their practice. This past year saw the twenty-fifth anniversary of the Core Program, prompting the MFAH to consider how this initiative has played a role in the larger art world. *Amy Blakemore: Photographs 1988–2008* is one of several projects the museum has undertaken to highlight this important landmark in our institutional history.

Arriving in 1985, Amy Blakemore was among the Core Program's early residents, and she has recalled: "I think I learned more in those two years than at any other time in my life. It certainly sent me in a direction…that I never would have imagined or considered." Much as this residency gave direction to Blakemore, she has in turn given direction to Houston. Among the Core fellows who elected to remain in this city after their residency was complete, Blakemore is one of those who quietly has made an enormous difference. She joined the Glassell School faculty in 1986, and over the past two decades not only has she steered the school's expanding commitment to teaching photography, she has also emerged as an important mentor, bringing to her classes the rigorous eye and creative intuition that informs all her work. Independent of the MFAH, she has also established a career that has brought her both national and international recognition.

One way to measure the impact Blakemore has had on our community is the wide-ranging support this exhibition and catalogue have attracted, and major donors have come together as the "Friends of Amy Blakemore" to make this project possible. Their names appear on the sponsors page, and I would like to salute them for their leadership role in this endeavor. Additionally, many former students and friends have made contributions as well, and they too are cited with gratitude.

I would also like to acknowledge the museum's supporters who have made it possible for the MFAH to assemble a permanent document of Blakemore's